The Zebra Who Lost His Stripes

Eddie the zebra was happy, the rain had finally stopped and the sun was shining over the jungle.

'Mama, please can I go outside to play with my friends, please?!' said Eddie.

'Yes,' said his mother, 'but Eddie, you stick to the path, the jungle is still very wet and very, very muddy.'

'OK,' said Eddie, and off he went.

But once outside in the warm sunshine Eddie was so excited that he forgot all that his Mama had said and went skipping off right through the middle of the jungle.

He had so much fun sliding down the huge leaves, rolling in the tall grass and splashing in the enormous muddy puddles! Eddie got very, very muddy!

Finally he saw his friends and went running over.

'Hello' said Eddie.

'Who are you?' asked one of the zebras.

'It's me, Eddie the zebra,' he said.

'You're not a zebra, you haven't got any stripes, you're all brown!'

Eddie looked down at himself. It was true! His stripes had disappeared!

'So said the other zebra, 'You can't play with us if you are not a zebra. Go away!'

Poor Eddie was so upset that he ran all the way home crying.

'Mama! Mama!' cried Eddie.

'What's the matter, Eddie?' said his Mama.

'The other zebras wouldn't let me play because I have lost my stripes and I'm not a zebra!' sobbed Eddie.

'Well,' said his Mama, 'Now listen to me Eddie, you are and always will be a zebra, but if your stripes are so important to you, follow me.'

So Eddie sniffed and wiped away his tears and followed his Mama to the big lake where all the animals drank from, but, instead of stopping at the water's edge his Mama walked all the way in ...

'Come on Eddie,' she said.

So Eddie did as he was told and followed his Mama, splashing and swimming across the lake and back again, and when he got out .....

'Look Mama! My stripes are back! I am a zebra after all!'

His Mama smiled and said, ' I know, my darling, I know'

The End